SNAILS

SNAILS

by Sylvia A. Johnson

Photographs by Modoki Masuda

A Lerner Natural Science Book

Lerner Publications Company ▪ Minneapolis

Sylvia A. Johnson, Series Editor

Translation of original text by Chaim Uri

Additional research by Jane Dallinger

Additional photographs by: p. 5 (top), Atsushi Sakurai; p. 5 (center), Isao Kishida; p. 30, Yuko Sato; p. 33, H. Paul Shank, Tom Stack & Associates; p. 42, Klaus Paysan; pp. 43, 45 (upper left, lower), A. Kerstitch, Tom Stack & Associates; p. 45 (upper right), Ed Robinson, Tom Stack & Associates. Cover photograph by Dave Spier, Tom Stack & Associates.

The publisher wishes to thank Dale A. Chelberg, former Curator of Biology, The Science Museum of Minnesota, for his assistance in the preparation of this book.

The glossary on page 46 gives definitions and pronunciations of words shown in **bold type** in the text.

LIBRARY OF CONGRESS CATALOGING IN PUBLICATION DATA

Johnson, Sylvia A.
   Snails.

   (A Lerner natural science book)
   Adaptation of: Katatsumuri/by Yasuyuki Koike.
   Includes index.
   Summary: An introduction to the structure and way of life of some of the 40,000 kinds of snails, with an emphasis on land snails.
   1. Snails—Juvenile literature. [1. Snails] I. Masuda, Modoki, ill. II. Koike, Yasuyuki. Katatsumuri. III. Title. IV. Series.
   QL430.4.J58   1982   594′.3   82-10086
   ISBN 0-8225-1475-3 (lib. bdg.)

International Standard Book Number: 0-8225-1475-3
Library of Congress Catalog Card Number: 82-10086

   3   4   5   6   7   8   9   10   90   89   88   87   86   85   84

If you wanted to see a snail, where would you look? You might look in a damp corner of your basement or under dead leaves on the forest floor. Some snails can be found high up in trees, while others live among garden plants. A great many snails make their homes in bodies of water—in ponds, lakes, and especially in the oceans. There are at least 40,000 kinds of snails, and they have many different ways of life. This book presents an introduction to land snails, like the ones shown in the pictures on the right. It also takes a look at a few of the fascinating snails that live in a watery environment.

Opposite: Like most other kinds of snails, this land snail can pull its whole body inside its beautiful, spiral-shaped shell.

There are many differences between land snails and those that live in water, but most snails have some basic features in common. Snails belong to a large group, or phylum, of animals known as **mollusks.** Mollusks have soft bodies, and many of them have shells during some stage in their lives. These are important characteristics of most snails. Mollusks like oysters and clams are called **bivalves** because they have two shells, joined together by a kind of hinge. Snails are **univalves,** animals with only one shell.

Gastropod is another scientific name for snails that describes one of the animals' important features. The term comes from two Greek words meaning "belly-foot." Snails were given this name because they seem to walk on their bellies.

Actually, a snail's body is put together in such an unusual way that terms like "belly" and "foot" don't have much meaning. A snail's "foot"—it has only one—is the long, flat piece of tissue and muscle on which the animal crawls. Joined to the front end of the foot is the snail's head, equipped with a mouth, eyes, and sense organs called **tentacles.** Most of a snail's internal organs are located in a kind of hump that fits inside the shell.

Later in this book, we will take a closer look at the parts of a snail's body. Right now, let's see how this strange little animal lives in its natural environment.

When spring rains fall and flowers bloom in fields and forests, land snails become active.

If you live in an area with a temperate climate, spring is the best time of year to see land snails. The animals spend the winter in the inactive state of **hibernation,** but the first warm rains of spring bring them out of their hiding places. Moisture is very important in the life of a snail. If its soft body is not kept moist, the snail will die.

When the sun shines, snails stay in damp, shady places under rocks and logs. If you want to see snails active and moving, you must look for them on rainy days or at night, when everything is wet with dew.

8

Above: A land snail feeding on tender tree leaves
Opposite: Two snails meet on a log in the forest.

The first thing that a snail does when it comes out on a wet spring day is to look for food. While they are in hibernation, snails do not eat, so they are very hungry when they become active in the spring. Most land snails are plant eaters, feeding on the tender new leaves and buds of trees and shrubs. Some snails also eat dead and decaying plant material.

To reach its favorite foods, a snail moves slowly over the ground or along plant stems using its muscular foot. A special gland in the foot produces a liquid called **mucus** that helps a snail to glide along. Most snails move at a slow "snail's pace" because their shells are large and heavy in proportion to their small bodies.

Like snails, tree frogs are active in the spring and can often be seen on rainy days.

12

For land snails, tree frogs, and many other animals, spring is the time of year for mating. Finding mates and producing young are important parts of the lives of most animals. The way in which land snails reproduce is unusual and fascinating.

Like frogs, birds, humans, and many other living things, land snails create more of their own kind through the process of sexual reproduction. New land snails are formed by the union of special sex cells known as **eggs** and **sperm.** In most kinds of animals, there are two separate sexes that produce the two different kinds of sex cells inside their bodies. Male animals produce sperm, and female animals produce eggs. But most land snails are not divided into two separate sexes. They are **hermaphrodites,** animals whose bodies manufacture both eggs and sperm.

Even though one land snail produces both male and female sex cells, it cannot reproduce all by itself. A snail's eggs must be united with another snail's sperm in order for new life to begin. When it comes time to mate, land snails must find partners just as frogs and birds do. The job is simpler for a land snail, however, since it does not have to look for a mate of the opposite sex. It can mate with any other snail that is a member of its own species.

Like many other animals, land snails often behave in special ways at the time of mating. Some snails, like the ones pictured here, have complicated courtship ceremonies that they use to identify each other and to get ready for mating. A snail looking for a mate will approach another snail

Left: Two snails begin the courtship that prepares them for mating. *Right:* The snails come close together and touch each other.

and move around it slowly in a circle. The two snails may rub their heads and feet together.

Many land snails that belong to the large group called Helicacea have a very unusual courtship ceremony. Sometime before mating, each snail jabs its partner with a small, sharp dart. These tiny darts are made of a shell-like material and are produced in special sacs inside the snails' bodies. Scientists are not sure why the snails jab each other in this strange way. Each species of Helicacea snail seems to produce darts of a different shape, so the jabbing may be a way for two snails to make sure that they have found the right partners. The darts may also serve to get the snails' bodies ready for the act of mating.

15

Above: After jabbing each other with sharp darts, the two snails exchange packets of sperm. *Left:* This picture shows one of the tiny "love-darts" that the snails use during their courtship.

A snail digging a hole
for its eggs

When land snails mate, they exchange sperm. First one snail deposits a packet of sperm in its partner's body through an opening near the head called the **genital pore.** Then the snail receives sperm from its partner in the same way. Inside each snail's body, the sperm unite with, or fertilize, the eggs, and mating is complete.

After they have mated, the two snails separate and go their own ways. About one month later, both are ready to lay their eggs. Many kinds of land snails lay their eggs in damp soil. A snail uses its head to push aside the dirt and make a hole about four inches (10 centimeters) deep. Other land snails lay their eggs under rocks, dead leaves, or the bark of trees.

The snail's eggs come out of its body through the genital pore. Each egg is tiny, less than ⅛ inch (about 3 millimeters) in diameter. The snail shown in these pictures lays about 50 eggs at one time; other land snails may lay several hundred. After the eggs have been deposited in the hole, the snail pushes the dirt over them and smooths it out. Then it leaves the eggs to develop on their own.

Opposite: **A snail's eggs leave its body through the genital pore.** *Right:* **A baby snail developing inside its egg.**

Inside each egg, a tiny new snail is growing. It is nourished by the food material contained in the part of the egg called the yolk. The egg's tough, jelly-like covering protects the growing snail from injury.

At this early stage of its development, the little snail is called an **embryo,** a name used to describe many kinds of animals during the period before birth or hatching. The time that it takes for snail embryos to develop varies from species to species. The species of snail pictured here spends three to four weeks inside its egg. During this period, the little snail's shell begins to take shape. By the time the snail is ready to hatch, you can see the tiny coiled shell through the egg's jelly covering (above).

When the eggs are ready to hatch, small cracks begin to appear in their coverings. The cracks soon widen, and the baby snails stick their heads out. A few minutes later, the coverings of the eggs break open, and the snails emerge.

19

Opposite: Land snails that have just hatched from their eggs. *Right:* This baby snail is getting ready to eat the tender shoot of a young plant.

The new little snails look very much like their parents, except that their bodies and shells are much smaller. A baby snail's shell is soft and thin, but as the snail grows, the shell will become harder and thicker. It will also become larger by adding more and more coiled sections, or **whorls**.

In order to grow into adults, baby snails need a lot of food. Their first meal usually consists of the soft shells of their empty eggs. Then the snails look for green plants to eat. They particularly like the tender shoots and leaves of young plants.

At first, the little snails stay near the place where they hatched, but soon they crawl away to continue their search for food.

Let's take a closer look at a young land snail as it begins its active life. The snail in the picture on the opposite page is about one month old. Its shell has been growing and already has more whorls than the shells of the newly hatched snails shown on page 20.

The growth of a snail's shell is a strange and fascinating process. The shell is produced by a thin skin or membrane called the **mantle,** which covers the top part of the snail's body under the shell. Glands in the mantle manufacture the hard material of the shell, using chemicals in the water and food that the snail consumes. New material is added to the edge or lip of the shell, behind the snail's head. As more and more shell material is produced by the mantle, new whorls are formed and the shell grows larger.

As it grows, a snail's shell forms a kind of cone-shaped spiral. Each new whorl of the spiral is larger than the one before it and overlaps the earlier whorl at a slightly lower level. Many land snails have shells shaped like flattened cones, but the shells of other snails, like the one shown on page 33, form long, deep cones with points at the ends.

The highest point of a snail's cone-shaped shell is called its **apex.** This is the oldest section of the shell since it formed first in the snail's development. The newest section of the shell is the large **body whorl** out of which the snail's head and foot emerge.

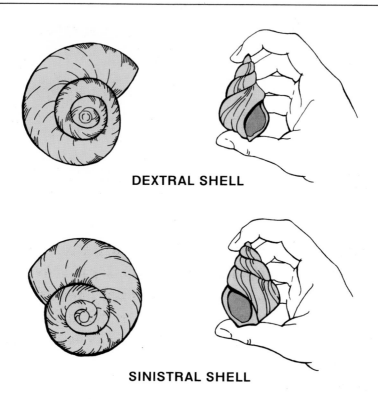

DEXTRAL SHELL

SINISTRAL SHELL

The spirals of most snail shells turn in a clockwise direction. Beginning with the first whorl, the spiral always coils to the right. Shells formed in this way are called right-handed or *dextral* shells. There are a few kinds of snails that have left-handed or *sinistral* shells, which coil counterclockwise.

You can tell if a snail shell is right-handed or left-handed by holding the shell with the apex at the top and the opening in the body whorl facing you. The opening of a dextral shell will be on the right, while the opening of a sinistral shell will be on the left.

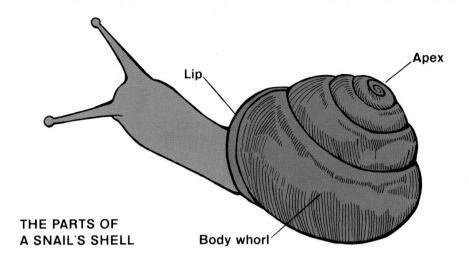

Apex

Lip

**THE PARTS OF
A SNAIL'S SHELL**

Body whorl

What is underneath the coiled shell that a snail carries with it wherever it goes? Within the largest whorl is located the snail's **visceral hump,** the part of its body containing most of the internal organs, or viscera. Just as the shell grows in a twisting spiral shape, the visceral hump also twists and turns as the snail develops.

This twisting or **torsion** starts when the snail is still in its egg. As the developing shell begins to coil in a spiral, the visceral hump twists along with it. The hump and the organs inside it turn in a half circle. When this happens, the organs that were originally in the back of the snail's body move around to the front. The snail's digestive system develops a U-turn, and the opening from which waste material is expelled moves around to a position near the snail's head.

Torsion gives the snail a kind of lopsided structure that is unique in the animal world. It makes the snail's anatomy rather difficult to understand, but snails seem to have no problem living with their twisted bodies and shells.

A two-month-old snail and an adult crawl along a pole on a rainy day. Like some of the other snails shown in this book, these two snails have left-handed or sinistral shells. If you look closely at the adult snail, you can see that the coils of its shell turn counterclockwise. Left-handed snails are not very common. Most land and marine snails have right-handed shells.

27

Most kinds of land snails have four tentacles, with eyes located at the tips of the two longest tentacles.

A snail's visceral hump is always hidden inside the shell, but other important parts of its body can be seen from the outside. If you look at the back of a land snail's head, you will notice two pairs of stalks or tentacles. The snail's eyes are located on the tips of the longer pair of tentacles. Scientists believe that the eyesight of most snails is not very good. A snail can tell the difference between light and dark, but it probably can't see clear images.

This series of pictures shows a snail pulling in its tentacles.

The two shorter tentacles may be more useful in providing the snail with information about its surroundings. These tentacles are sensitive to touch, and the snail uses them to feel objects in its path.

Both sets of tentacles can be moved around in all directions. They can also be pulled inside the snail's head, as these pictures show. A snail will usually pull in, or retract, its tentacles when it is frightened by something. The tentacles seem to collapse inward as if they were being pulled from the inside (top and center). The tentacles become shorter and shorter until they finally disappear inside the snail's head (bottom).

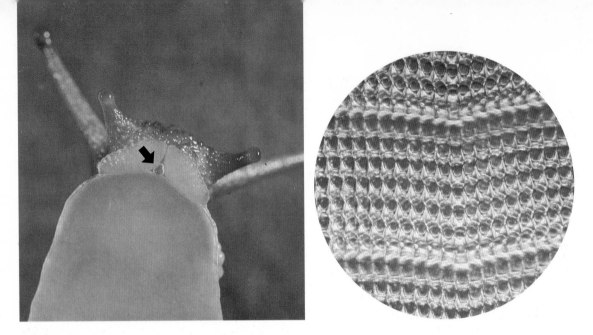

Left: A snail's mouth. *Right:* The tiny teeth on the tongue-like radula, shown enlarged many times.

A snail's mouth is located on the front of its head. Inside the mouth is a special organ called the **radula.** A snail's radula is a kind of long, flat tongue covered with rows of tiny, sharp teeth. When a snail eats, it extends the radula and moves it back and forth like a little file. The sharp teeth on the radula scrape off pieces of food material, which the snail then pulls into its mouth.

After the food has passed through the snail's digestive system, waste material leaves the snail's body through the **anal opening.** Because of the torsion or twisting of the snail's organs, this opening is at the front of the body rather than at the back, as it would be in most other kinds of animals.

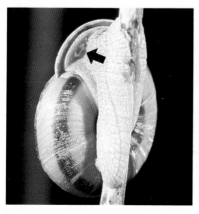

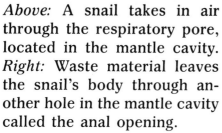

Above: A snail takes in air through the respiratory pore, located in the mantle cavity. *Right:* Waste material leaves the snail's body through another hole in the mantle cavity called the anal opening.

The anal opening is located in a space under the edge of the shell called the **mantle cavity.** Within this space, the mantle forms a kind of fold, and the anal opening comes out through this fold.

Next to the anal opening in the mantle cavity is a larger opening called the **respiratory pore.** Through this hole, the snail takes air into its body. The respiratory pore is connected to the snail's lungs, which draw oxygen from the air and expel the waste gas carbon dioxide. All land snails breathe through lungs, but most snails that live in water have gills something like those of fish.

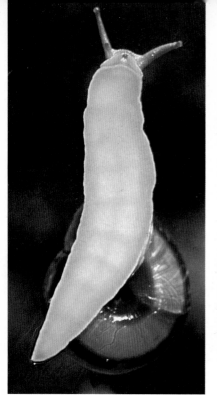

Left: The bottom of a snail's foot seen through a piece of glass. The faint horizontal lines are caused by the muscle contractions that move the snail forward. *Right:* A snail uses its versatile foot to crawl up a thin vine.

A snail's foot is the largest part of its body that can be seen outside the shell. On this long, flat piece of tissue, a snail can move from place to place with great ease. The bottom of the foot contains many muscles that provide the power to move the snail along its way. These muscles contract, or tighten, in waves that travel from the back of the foot to the front. When the contractions reach the front of the foot, they push it forward. As the contractions follow one after another, they move the snail along in a slow, graceful glide.

32

Another thing that helps a land snail to move easily is the mucus produced by its foot. This slippery liquid comes from a gland at the front of the foot. The mucus forms a kind of path that the snail glides over as it moves. A trail of mucus is left behind after the snail has passed by.

When a snail is not using its foot to move along the ground or cling to a branch, it may pull this part of its body inside the shell. Both the foot and the head are connected to strong muscles that are attached to the inside of the shell. Using these muscles, a snail can draw its whole body up into the interior of the protective shell.

This tree snail has drawn most of its body inside its shell. Only the front of its head is sticking out.

A glowworm eating a snail

Snails usually withdraw into their shells when their instincts tell them that danger threatens. Unfortunately, shells cannot protect land snails from some of the animals that hunt and eat them. Birds, frogs, toads, small mammals, and insects are among the many different creatures that prey on land snails. Some birds use their sharp, hooked beaks to reach inside a snail's shell and pull the occupant out. Other birds hold snails in their beaks and smash the shells against rocks until they break.

Snails make a juicy meal for several kinds of beetles. Ground beetles like the one shown on the opposite page have narrow, flexible heads that they can push deep inside a snail's shell. The firefly is a beetle that feeds on snails during its larval stage, before it has developed into an adult. Larval fireflies, known as glowworms, inject snails with a poison that turns their bodies into a liquid. The glowworms can then drink their dinner out of the snails' shells.

Human beings are also very fond of taking snails out of their shells and eating them. Some kinds of land snails are sold as food and are considered a delicacy in many parts of the world.

34

The ground beetle is another insect that preys on snails.

Above: A snail shell sealed with mucus. The tiny hole in the bottom part of the seal allows air to get into the shell. *Right:* This estivating snail has attached itself to a tree branch with mucus.

When a snail withdraws into its shell, it is often seeking protection not from predators but from the weather. During hot, dry periods, land snails hide inside their shells to keep their moist bodies from drying out. The shell opening is sealed by a thin film of mucus that is produced by the snail's body. This mucus becomes dry and hard, forming a tight covering that keeps moisture in. A tiny hole in the mucous seal lets air into the shell.

Inside its sealed shell, a snail rests quietly, waiting for better weather conditions. During this time, the snail does not eat, and its body functions slow down. It is in a state that scientists call **estivation.**

During long periods of dryness, an estivating snail may stay in its shell for several months. When moisture finally returns, the snail will break the shell seal and slowly emerge.

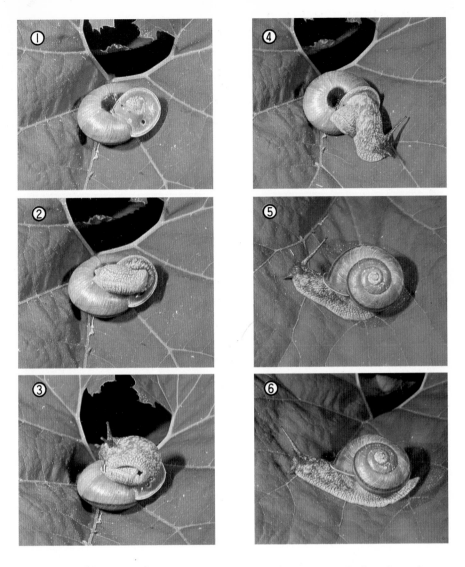

These pictures show the emergence of a snail that has been brought out of estivation by having water sprinkled on the seal of its shell. The snail pushes against the mucous seal from inside (1) until the seal breaks. Out comes part of the snail's foot (2) and then its head (3). After the snail pulls the rest of its foot out of the opening (4 and 5), it is ready to crawl away (6).

Above and opposite: Snails searching for food among brightly colored autumn leaves

Land snails that live in areas with temperate climates usually spend some part of the warm summer months in estivation. As the summer comes to an end and the leaves begin to change colors, snails get ready for an even longer period of inactivity. They will spend the cold winter in hibernation, securely sealed inside their shells.

To prepare for hibernation, snails eat as much as they can before the cold weather begins. They must store enough food energy in their bodies to get through the winter without eating.

Left: The mucous seal on this snail's shell is still soft and transparent. *Right:* These two shells are tightly sealed by tough, dry layers of mucus.

As the red and gold leaves drop from the trees and the temperature falls, land snails begin their final preparations for hibernation. Some snails burrow under dead leaves or into cracks in rocks. Others attach themselves to twigs and branches with sticky mucus. When a snail has found a good resting place, it begins to make a mucous seal for its shell. The seal is usually formed from several layers of mucus so that it will be tough enough to keep out the winter cold.

Shut tight in their shells, most land snails spend the winter in the sleep-like state of hibernation. They will not emerge again until spring comes with its mild temperatures and drenching rains.

The pond snail (left) and the ramshorn snail (right) are two common kinds of freshwater snails.

Snails that live in water do not have to depend on rain to keep their bodies moist. They are always surrounded by moisture. Some snails, like the ones shown above, make their homes in ponds, streams, and other bodies of fresh water. A few of these snails have gills, but most breathe through lungs, like land snails, and have to come to the surface of the water to take air into their bodies. Unlike land snails, freshwater snails have only one pair of tentacles, with their eyes located at the base of the tentacles. Most of these snails are plant-eaters, like their land-dwelling cousins.

There are large numbers of snails that live in the salty waters of the world's oceans. These **marine** snails have many things in common with land snails, but they have some special features of their own. One such feature is the **siphon,** a tube-like structure that sticks out at the front of a marine snail's shell. This tube, which is formed by the mantle, serves as a kind of hose, drawing water into the mantle cavity. A marine snail's gills are located in the mantle cavity, and they take dissolved oxygen from the water so that the snail can breathe.

In this picture of a helmet snail, you can see the tube-like siphon sticking out at the front of the colorful shell.

A feature shared by marine snails and some freshwater snails is the **operculum,** a kind of trap door used to close the opening of the snails' shells. The operculum is a horny plate that is part of a marine snail's foot. When the snail withdraws into its shell, this plate fits into the shell opening, sealing the snail inside.

The shells of marine snails come in a great variety of shapes and colors. Although they are formed in the same way as the shells of other snails, marine snail shells often look very different from the simple spirals that most land snails carry on their backs.

Some marine snails like the conches and the murex snails have shells with fantastic spikes and spines on their surfaces. Others like the cowries have smooth, glossy shells shaped something like chicken eggs. The shells of cone snails are long and narrow, while other marine snail shells are shaped like turbans, helmets, and screws.

The colors and markings of marine snail shells are as varied as their unusual shapes. Many cowries and cones have complicated patterns of stripes, dots, and splotches on the exteriors of their shells. The colors of the shells range from brilliant yellows and golds to elegant browns and blacks. Conch shells are not very colorful on the outside, but they are often lined with smooth, shining pink. The bodies of some marine snails are as brightly colored and intricately patterned as their shells.

44

The tiger cowry (left) and the Triton's trumpet (right) are two marine snails with beautifully patterned shells.

Many marine snails are predators that kill and eat other sea creatures. Some cone snails (left) inject their prey with a paralyzing poison. Murex snails (right) sometimes use the edges of their spiked shells to pry open the shells of scallops and other marine bivalves.

GLOSSARY

anal (AY-nuhl) opening—the opening in the mantle cavity through which waste material leaves a snail's body

apex (AY-pex)—the highest point of a snail's shell

bivalves—mollusks like oysters and clams that have two hinged shells

body whorl—the largest section of a snail's shell, out of which the head and foot emerge

dextral (DEX-truhl)—right-handed; used to describe a shell that coils in a clockwise direction

estivation (es-tih-VAY-shun)—a period of inactivity during hot, dry weather. At this time, an animal does not eat, and its body functions slow down.

gastropod (GAS-truh-pod)—a mollusk that belongs to the class Gastropoda. The term comes from two Greek words meaning "belly-foot."

genital (JEN-ih-tuhl) pore—an opening near a snail's head connected to the reproductive system

hermaphrodites (her-MAF-ruh-dites)—animals that produce both male and female sex cells

hibernation—a period of inactivity during cold weather

mantle (MAN-tuhl)—a thin membrane that produces the hard material of a snail's shell

mantle cavity—a space under the edge or lip of a snail's shell

marine snails—snails that live in the oceans

mollusks (MAHL-usks)—animals that belong to the phylum Mollusca. This group of soft-bodied creatures includes snails, oysters, and octopuses.

mucus (MYU-kus)—a slippery liquid produced by a snail's body and used for many different purposes

operculum (oh-PER-kyuh-lum)—a horny plate on the back part of a snail's foot. When the snail withdraws into its shell, the operculum fits into the shell opening.

radula (RAJ-uh-luh)—a tongue-like organ in a snail's mouth, covered with tiny teeth

respiratory (RES-pi-ruh-tor-ee) pore—an opening in the mantle cavity connected to a snail's lungs

sinistral (SIN-is-truhl)—left-handed; used to describe a snail shell that coils in a counterclockwise direction.

siphon (SI-fuhn)—a tube that sticks out of the mantle cavity of a marine snail

tentacles (TENT-ih-kuhls)—the stalks or feelers on a snail's head

torsion (TOR-shun)—the twisting of a snail's body caused by the coiling of the shell

univalves—mollusks with only one shell

visceral (VIS-uh-ruhl) hump—the part of a snail's body containing its internal organs

whorl—one of the coiled sections of a snail's shell

INDEX